Ryan ♡ Mama

Ryan ♡ Papa

Bear Facts Library™

HATS
THE BEARS
GREAT NATURAL BEAR'S LAIR
Welcome to Bear

FARMER BEN'S
MARKET
HONEY
ACTUAL
FACTUAL
BEAR
W
S
N
E
Country

The Berenstain Bears'
ALMANAC
A Year in Bear Country...
holidays
seasons
weather
actual facts about snow, wind, rain, thunder, lightning, the sun, the moon...
and
lots
more
by Stan and Jan Berenstain
Random House · New York

 Published in the United States by Random House, Inc., New York, and simultaneously in Canada by Random House of Canada Limited, Toronto. *Library of Congress Cataloging in Publication Data:* Berenstain, Stanley. The bears' almanac. SUMMARY: The further adventures of the Bear family also include information on holidays, weather, and the seasons. [1. Bears–Stories. 2. Seasons–Fiction. 3. Stories in rhyme] I. Berenstain, Janice, joint author. II. Title. PZ7.B4483Baf [Fic] 73-2298 ISBN: 0-394-82693-0 (trade hardcover); 0-394-92693-5 (library binding); 0-394-86601-0 (trade paperback) Manufactured in the United States of America 4

A Year in Bear Country

What makes a year?

Four Seasons. Four is all.
Winter, Spring, Summer, Fall.

Twelve Months. A lot to say.
January, February,
March, April, May.
June, July,
August, September.
October, November
and December.

How will you know
which season is here?
Come and we'll show you
a Bear Country year.

A brand-new calendar!
Hooray! Hooray!
A whole new year
starts today!

In the very first month
on the very first day . . .

is what we say.

The first three months of the year are WINTER

HOW WILL YOU KNOW IT'S WINTER?

Your knees shiver.

You see ice on the river.

Your breath shows.

You've got a
runny nose.

You have to wear a scarf and cap.

Great Natural Bear
starts his
LONG winter nap.

Good night, Small Bear.
See you next Spring.
GREAT NATURAL BEAR'S LAIR

Papa puts on long underwear.

There are
fat snowflakes in the air.

The red in the thermometer starts to fall.
Sometimes there's hardly any red at all.

Brrr!
IT'S WINTER!

ACTUAL FACTS ABOUT SNOW

When it's cold
the clouds freeze.
Clouds turn into flakes of ice.
The ice flakes fall . . .
That's **snow.**
Children think it's nice.

Some places have no snow,
you'll find.
Children there
don't seem to mind.

In sunny places
such as these,
it's just too hot
for clouds to freeze.

Sometimes snow
comes and goes in a hurry.

When snow does that . . .

it's called a **flurry.**

A blizzard . . .

That is what we call
a really, really
BIG snowfall.

You may see it flurry.
You may see it fly . . .
But there's more to snow
than meets the eye.

ACTUAL FACTUA BEAR

You are different
from your sisters and brothers.

And EVERY snowflake
is different from the others.

That is a very nice
thing to know
the next time you are
watching snow.

SOME OF THE THINGS WINTER BRINGS
snow shovel
snow blower
snow plow
snow thrower
snowballs in the air
Hey! Look out, Papa Bear!

sick in bed
nose drops
brand-new sled
belly flops
spinning wheels
snowmobiles
He can skate
a figure eight.
Say! Look what
she can do . . .
six thousand
nine hundred
thirty-two!

Still stuck.
tow truck
HOCKEY TODAY
stick
puck
goalie
goal
He is fishing through a hole.
barrel jump
1 2 3 4 5 6 7
ker-thump!

DEAD MAN'S HILL
What a spill!
ski run
ski lift
snowshoes
snowdrift
This snow is very, very deep.
Great Natural Bear is still asleep!
ZZZZZZZ
GREAT NATURAL BEAR'S LAIR

In February,
on Valentine's Day...

I LOVE YOU IS WHAT WE SAY

But . . . if you're shy . . .
GUESS WHO
will do.

GUESS WHO!
In MARCH, friends, Winter ends.

The next three months of the year are SPRING

HOW WILL YOU KNOW IT'S SPRING?

There is slush and mush
from melting snow.

Birds sing.
Plants grow.

A crocus grows
right through
the snow.

Wind blows hats off people's heads.

We take out bikes.
We put back sleds.

It's time to get out brooms and mops.

It starts to rain . . .

then it stops.

The sun begins
to warm the air.
Nice
day,
Small Bear.
Great Natural Bear
comes out
of his lair . . .
GREAT
NATURAL
BEAR'S
LAIR
Hooray!
IT'S SPRING!

The first day in April
is **APRIL FOOL'S DAY.**

Your friends will try
to fool you today.
Here are some of the
things they will say . . .

There's a bug
on your nose!

Your shoes
are not tied!

There's a hole
in your pants!

There's a big purple
monster outside!!

Of course there isn't
a bug
on your nose.

There's no hole
in your pants.

And your shoes
are both tied.

And as for big purple monsters . . .

Help! A big purple
monster is waiting
outside!

APRIL FOOL!

FLYING A KITE . . .

Is a very fine thing
that you and I
can do in Spring .

I'm ready, Dad.
Let me try it.
I'll take it out right now
and fly it!

Not yet, my boy.
Hold on, Son.
First I'll show you
how it's done.

Now, check the string.
You need a lot.
You also need
a windy spot.

But, Papa!
For a kite to sail...
doesn't it have
to have a tail?
Yes, Small Bear.
You are learning how.
This nice long tail
goes on right now!
Next, you must know
which way to run.
Watch the wind blow
and go that way, Son.

But, Dad!
Is that way right?
Shouldn't you run
the other way
with a kite?
Right! Here we go!
Hold the kite high!
I'll let out some string
and we'll let 'er fly!
I get it, Dad! . . .
Except for one thing.
Didn't you let out
too much string?

Son, I showed you
how to do it right.
Now why don't you just
go fly your kite?

What you will need.

A good strong kite.
Plenty of string.
A nice long tail.
A day in Spring.

ACTUAL FACTS ABOUT WIND

Air. Air.
It's everywhere.
When it moves
from here . . .
to there . . .
that's wind.
ACTUAL FACTUAL BEAR
The wind sails boats . . .
and paper planes.
It turns windmills . . .
and weather vanes.
A weather vane always shows just which way the wind blows.
W
N
E
S

A soft, soft wind
blows the trees....
A soft, soft wind
is called a **breeze**.

But...
Sometimes the wind
is so strong that
it blows off
Farmer Ben Bear's hat.

It blows away
his stool and pail....
THAT kind of wind
is called a **gale**.

A **tornado.**

A **tornado!**

That's when
the big wind lifts
poor Farmer Ben.
It lifts him, cow and all,
and then . . .
It whirls him round
and round again.

It's kind of hard
on Farmer Ben.

ACTUAL FACTS ABOUT RAIN

There are drops of water
in the clouds.
They are very, very small.
When they get together,
they get big enough
to fall.
That's **rain**.

When just a few
drops fall,
a **drizzle** is what you get.
A drizzle isn't much ....
You don't get very wet.

When more
drops fall,
a **shower**
is what you get.
A shower makes you
very wet.

When millions of drops
pour down
a **downpour** is what you get.

A downpour
makes you
SOAKING
wet.

After the rain,
sometimes
a **rainbow** is what you get.

A rainbow is worth
all that wet.

SOME OF THE THINGS SPRING BRINGS
eggs hatching
bear scratching
Mama cleaning
Brother sweeping
Sister painting
Papa sleeping
pulling weeds
planting seeds
Corn
Peas
Beans
Potatoes
Cabbage
Carrots
Beets
Tomatoes
jumping rope
rolling hoop
I'm waiting for some vegetable soup!

Easter eggs
jelly beans
Eating red ones.
Eating greens.
I just bit a chocolate bunny.
I don't think that's very funny!
Another thing Spring brings . . .
is BABIES!
baby rabbits
baby squirrels . . .
eleven boys, seven girls
Cats have kittens.
Dogs have puppies.
Hi, there! We are baby guppies!
Mama frog and her tads swim among the lily pads.
Hens have chicks. She has six.
Ducks have ducklings.
She has nine.
I'm a baby porcupine.
Coming soon: Spring ends in JUNE

The next three months of the year are

HOW WILL YOU KNOW IT'S SUMMER?

There's no more school.

Papa's in the swimming pool.

Mama's making
lemonade.

Granny's sitting
in the shade.

Mosquitoes bite.

You go to bed when
it's still light.

Everybody's very lazy . . .

except for plants.

They grow like crazy.

The red in the
thermometer
shoots up tall.
There's hardly any
room at all.

Phew!
IT'S SUMMER!

ACTUAL FACTS ABOUT THE SUN

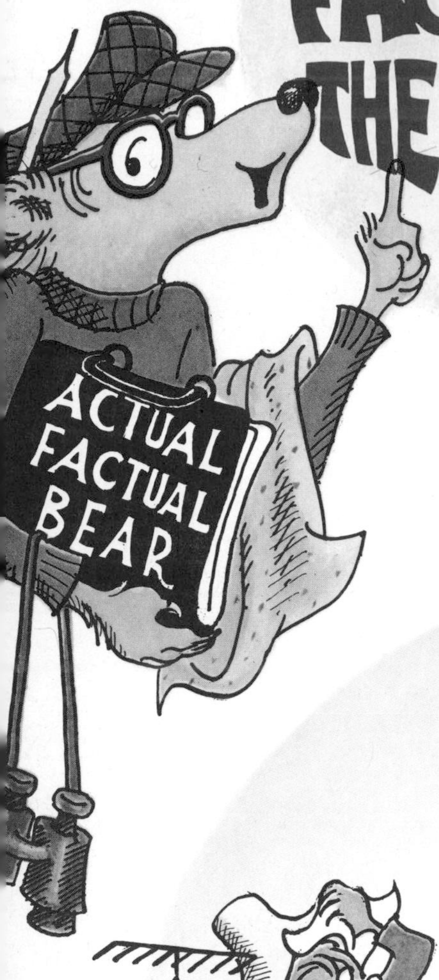

ACTUAL FACTUAL BEAR

The sun
is millions
of miles away.
But it works for us
every day.

Farmer Ben's plants
need light and heat
to grow into things
we like to eat.

Sun makes wheat
and corn grow tall.

Without it,
they would not grow
at all.

There would be

no peas . . .

or beans . . .

. . . or tomatoes.

We wouldn't even
have potatoes.

The sun helps potatoes
grow fat and round . . .
even though
they're
underground.

The sun can turn a seed this small into a sunflower ten feet tall!

The sun warms ponds
where fish eggs hatch.
And gives me lots of fish to catch.
The sun warms turtles.
It warms frogs.
We love to lie on sunny logs.
Bats and owls
stay out of it.
We don't like the sun one bit.

It's good for lying in hammocks . . . .

And splashing under hoses . . . .

But don't stay out in the sun too long . . .

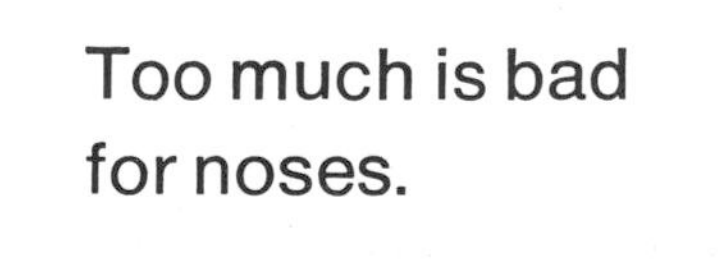
Too much is bad for noses.

JULY
4
INDEPENDENCE DAY
On July the fourth . . .
Cannons
boom!
Rockets
fly!
Pinwheels spin!

Fireworks fill the sky!

Why?

Because July the fourth is THE FOURTH OF JULY

It is also known as

INDEPENDENCE DAY

And on this day, we all say . . .

HAPPY BIRTHDAY USA

SUMMER BRINGS SUN AND FUN
swimming
floating
diving
boating
A bite! Look!
tanning
fanning
No hook!
outdoor cook

ball
bat
straw hat
Papa feels a little sick.
Too much watermelon!
Hic!
hot dogs
mustard
frozen custard
French fries
pies
Who invited all those flies?
ants
ants
ants
ants
You can't have a picnic without ants!
Look out! Here comes a thundercloud.
PLEASE! NO LITTERBUGS ALLOWED!

ACTUAL FACTS ABOUT THUNDER AND LIGHTNING

Electricity
in your home
lights your lights.
It runs
the vacuum
for your mother.

Electricity
in the clouds
shoots
giant sparks
from one cloud
to another.

That's **lightning**.

Sometimes it's
pretty frightening.

When lightning flashes
from cloud to cloud,
it makes a noise
that's VERY loud.

If you wonder . . .
That's **thunder**.

Something
to remember:
Summer ends
in September.

The next three months of the year are FALL

HOW WILL YOU KNOW IT'S FALL?

This is the time
of the Harvest Moon . . .

The time when the
caterpillar
makes his cocoon.

The weather
turns a little cool.

Some of us
are back in school.

Birds flying south
fill the sky.

Summer plants
turn brown and dry.

There are lots
of pumpkins
and apples around.

There is a red and gold
carpet of leaves
on the ground.

So it must be
FALL!

ACTUAL FACTS ABOUT THE MOON

FULL MOON

Sometimes the moon
is round and bright.
It lights the way
for us at night.

CRESCENT MOON

On other nights
the moon is slim.
There is light.
But the light is dim.

NO MOON

It gets very, very dark
when there is no moon in sight.

If you go out
on nights like these,
be sure to take a light.

The moon looks like
a smooth round ball.
But a close look will show you
the moon's not smooth at all.

Some day soon,
you may go
to the moon .
You'll wave good-bye
to your father and mother . . . .

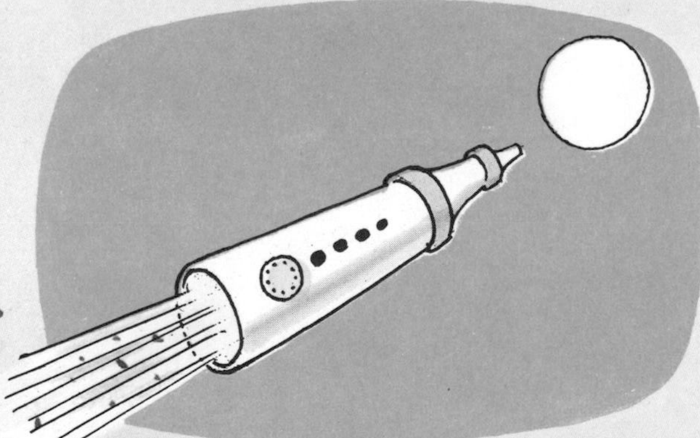

You'll rocket to the moon . . .

and get a moon rock
for your brother.

It's New Year's Eve!
A whole year ends.

Tomorrow we'll
start
a NEW YEAR,
friends.

So, now, we can
all turn back
to the beginning
of our Almanac.